*I'm Here to Learn to Dream in Your Language*

*I'm Here to Learn to Dream in Your Language*

H. L. Hix

etruscan press

Etruscan Press
Wilkes University
84 West South Street
Wilkes-Barre, PA 18766
(570) 408-4546

WILKES UNIVERSITY

www.etruscanpress.org

Published 2015 by Etruscan Press
Printed in the United States of America
Cover design by Laurie Powers
Cover image: Kyoung Ae Cho, "Pine Ball II"
Interior design and typesetting by Julianne Popovec
The text of this book is set in Arno Pro.

First Edition

15 16 17 18 19 5 4 3 2 1

                    Library of Congress Cataloging-in-Publication Data
Hix, H. L.
  [Poems. Selections]
  I'm here to learn to dream in your language / H. L. Hix.
    p. cm.
  ISBN 978-0-9897532-0-3 (pbk.)
  I. Title.
  PS3558.I88A6 2015
  811'.54--dc23
                    2014018567

*Please turn to the back of this book for a list of the sustaining funders of Etruscan Press.*

# I'm Here to Learn to Dream in Your Language

# AUSPICES

Paisley Rekdal

In H. L. Hix's aphoristic poem "Ice Bridge", one of the lines reads simply: "And a syntax that contested grammar." These poems take that fragment to heart: Hix's syntax is unlike that of any other poet I know working right now: they never sacrifice grammatical meaning for mere verbal play but make language twist and turn upon itself, not to shear sense from sound but to investigate how sound itself might become meaning. Like dreams, these poems shift subtly between lyric narratives, metanarratives, myths and aphoristic sound poems, anchored by the masterful long collage-poem "Dream Logic" in which each section responds to and draws upon the work of a different contemporary poet, creating a multi-vocal poem that both questions and redefines the idea of authorship. Where other poets try to hone one voice, one perspective over the course of a collection, Hix is more engaged with seeing how one mind can contain a thousand possibilities. It's an urge that structures the book as a whole, so that each long poem adds to the conversation, creating a collage of identities, a multi-hyphenated mind continually at work. In Hix's beautiful poems, language and thought become physical as well as abstract realities, where one dream can split off into a thousand dreamers, and a mouth can be "incised with Aeschylus....infused with Aegean salt."

Dan Beachy-Quick

In this set of sustained, sustaining, lyrical investigations, H. L. Hix puts on the mantle of his own poetic charge: to "invent new ways, by building new spaces, in which / to question." Such newly built spaces should not be confused with those conceptual architectures impervious to feeling. Far from it. Hix opens himself to the vulnerabilities the poems sense and seek. The poet doesn't say how it is he feels, but more profoundly asks that more difficult question: "What do I feel like?" Such wondering, such wonderment, returns us to the bewildered state in which the mind understands itself only through the uncomfortable intimacy between it and all things it must learn and re-learn to recognize, and so we find, as Hix finds, that our relation to ourselves as well as to every other—be it book or be it person, be it world or be it lover—is an act of translation desperate to discover the nature of its own faithfulness. To read *I'm Here to Learn to Dream in Your Language* is to realize that we have among us a visionary devoted to revelation. But what is there to be revealed save what already exists?—translated anew, ever anew, as the eye dilates to light before the mind translates the experience as "light." Then we know what is always has been. Such a poet is Hix—perhaps, among us, the primary poet of such work. Commenting beautifully—for he has not forsaken beauty as its own troubling intelligence—on all that already has past, so that we don't forget the past tense is the ongoing persuasion within all that now is and will be. I want to ask a simple question. Am I grateful for this work? I want to give a simple answer: Yes. I am abundantly grateful. And for what new readers discover Hix's poems in this volume, so simply I want to say: welcome, enter, abide: join the wide-eyed lot of us.

## Acknowledgments

The epigraphs to the sections come from, respectively: Alexander Blok, "Nature and Culture"; John Keats, "La Belle Dame sans Merci"; Lyn Hejinian, in Hejinian and Leslie Scalapino, *Sight*; Herman Melville, *Moby Dick*; Marilynne Robinson, *Housekeeping*.

"Dream Legend" is in immediate and particular dialogue with Jane Yeh, to whom I am most grateful. As I am grateful to Caleb Klaces for arranging that dialogue and publishing it at *Likestarlings.com*.

"Dream Lullaby" is in immediate and particular dialogue with the photograph around which Thomas E. Kennedy and Walter Cummins built their anthology *The Girl with Red Hair*, in which "Marie, Beside the River" was first published.

Each octave in "Dream Logic" is in immediate and particular dialogue with a book, and each matched sestet with an interview, by one of the following writers. The interviews in question all are posted at www.hlhix.com: click on the red IN QUIRE button, and then the Q&A button. I am grateful to these writers for their willingness to engage in such a dialogue: Paige Ackerson-Kiely, Dan Beachy-Quick, Tim Bowling, John Bradley, Lily Brown, Julie Bruck, David Caplan, Jared Carter, Heather Christle, Gillian Conoley, Matthew Cooperman, Renée E. D'Aoust, Jehanne Dubrow, Camille Dungy, Lisa Fishman, Andy Fitch, T Fleischmann, Veronica Golos, Janice Gould, Andrew Grace, Julie Hanson, Robert Hedin, Warren Heiti, Brian Henderson, David Hernandez, Karl Jirgens, Kirsten Kaschock, Scott King, Willie James King, Jacqueline Jones LaMon, Eleanor Lerman, Jessica Helen Lopez, Jill Magi, Barbara Maloutas, Valerie Martínez, Kristi Maxwell, Aaron McCollough, Shane McCrae, James Meetze, Philip Metres, Jenny Mueller, Nathanaël, Uche Nduka, Jena Osman, Alicia Suskin Ostriker, Danielle Pafunda, Lia Purpura, Paisley Rekdal, Karen Rigby, Elizabeth Robinson, Zach Savich, Don Share, Eleni Sikelianos, Sandra Simonds, Sue Sinclair, Johanna Skibsrud, Juliana Spahr, Catherine Taylor, Brian Teare, Sally Van Doren, Kathleen Wakefield, Jon Woodward, Laurie Saurborn Young, Jan Zwicky.

"Dream Lexicon" is in immediate and particular dialogue with *Moby Dick* and the *Oxford English Dictionary*.

Each poem in "Dream Longing" is in immediate and particular dialogue with a poem in translation. I am grateful to the poets who wrote those poems, to the translators who gave the poems to those of us unable to read them in their original languages, and to the publishers who engaged in the unprofitable but profoundly important labor of presenting poetry in translation to an English-speaking audience.

The poems with which these poems are privileged to converse were written by: Nazik al-Malaika, Adnan Al-Sayegh, Ece Ayhan, Ilhan Berk, Astrid Cabral, Edip Cansever, Sigitas Geda, Joumana Haddad, Hsüeh Ch'iung, Mohja Kahf, Kang Ûngyo, Ingrid de Kok, Srecko Kosovel, Omar Pérez López, Sonia Manzano, Antonio Preciado, Andrzej Sosnowski, Cemal Süreya, Wang Wei, Yi Chinmyông, Yi Sanghui, Ghassan Zaqtan, Mustafa Zvizdic.

The poems in question appear in translation in the following books:

Agee, Chris, ed. *Scar on the Stone: Contemporary Poetry from Bosnia.* Bloodaxe, 1998.

Berk, Ilhan. *A Leaf About to Fall: Selected Poems.* Trans. George Messo. Salt Publishing, 2006.

Cabral, Astrid. *Cage.* Trans. Alexis Levitin. Host Publications, 2008.

Geda, Sigitas. *Biopsy of Winter.* Trans. Kerry Shawn Keys. Vaga, 2002.

Haddad, Joumana. *Invitation to a Secret Feast: Selected Poems.* Ed. Khaled Mattawa. Tupelo Press, 2008.

Handal, Nathalie, ed. *The Poetry of Arab Women: A Contemporary Anthology.* Interlink Books, 2001.

Hirson, Denis, ed. *The Lava of this Land: South African Poetry, 1960-1996.* Triquarterly Books, 1997.

Lee, Peter H., ed. *Echoing Song: Contemporary Korean Women Poets.* White Pine Press, 2005.

Levitin, Alexis, and Fernando Iturburu, ed. and trans. *Tapestry of the Sun: An Anthology of Ecuadorian Poetry.* Coimbra Editions, 2009.

Messo, George, ed. and trans. *Ikinci Yeni: The Turkish Avant-Garde.* Shearsman Books, 2009.

Mohammed, Sadek, et al., eds. *Flowers of Flame: Unheard Voices of Iraq.* Michigan St. Univ. Press, 2008.

Pribac, Bert, and David Brooks, trans. *The Golden Boat: Selected Poems of Srecko Kosovel*. Salt, 2008.

Rexroth, Kenneth, and Ling Chung, ed. and transl. *Women Poets of China*. New Directions, 1982.

Sosnowski, Andrzej. *Lodgings: Selected Poems*. Open Letter, 2011.

Weiss, Mark, ed. *The Whole Island: Six Decades of Cuban Poetry*. Univ. of California Press, 2009.

Zaqtan, Ghassan. *Like a Straw Bird It Follows Me, and Other Poems*. Trans. Fady Joudah. Yale Univ. Press, 2012.

My thanks to the editors of the following journals, who granted prior publication to versions of certain of the poems presented here: *Agni, Alabama Literary Review, Better, Borderlands, Connotation Press: An Online Artifact, Crazyhorse, december, DIAGRAM, Great River Review, Hotel Amerika, I-70 Review, McSweeney's, the minnesota review, The Nepotist, Offending Adam, Open Window Review, Poetry, Poetry Northwest, Prosopisia, The Seattle Review, Think, Water~Stone Review, The Yale Review*.

I am deeply grateful to Paisley Rekdal and Dan Beachy-Quick for speaking on behalf of this work.

A few of the poems also bear dedications. "Sometimes I want what I want, but not often" is for Hubert. "What speaks heat must have been spoken by grit" is for Joy Williams. The opening and closing poems of "Dream Longing" are for Kate.

*I'm Here to Learn to Dream in Your Language*

# Dream Legend

*They, the elemental people, dream and create legends about the earth.*

## Thinking of Perfection

as gone before given, given as something other than itself,
by someone other than the giver, gives me over

to the stranger who slept with her head on my shoulder
half the flight, Detroit to Dublin, overnight,
nineteen-ninety-too-late-to-stop-the-rot-but-too-early-to-know.

To the circle of sunlight, reflected off the watchface
of a woman in a meeting, magnifying on the wall
and ceiling each least gesture of a wrist I could not see.

As what offers truth but will not suffer reality.

To the rasp of my steps over fresh snow loud against
the silence only mountain-town cold, the loneliness
only three a.m., can make so otherwise utter.

To the lilac blossoms, months past now and ever
months ahead, that overwhelm even longest winter.

As what, because it never began, need not end:
the stranger's mouthing *thank you* across the baggage carousel,
my waving at her back as she walked to passport control.

# What Is the Length and Purpose of Your Visit?

Let home still be home for others.

As design, this began with a gesture. As hope, well…

Spring, risen from roots; autumn, descended from branches.
No crocuses yet, just last year's leaves matted by snowmelt, most way to mud.

Last time my favorite word was "effortless." This time, "spared."

Overhearing is sexier here where I don't speak.

On walls, the same tags everywhere, but on boxcars a lexicon.
Is that security camera named for what it gives or what it takes away?

Missions. Flew a hundred successful. He. Meaning by "successful" what?

Wait here.

There were two of us last time.

"Effortless*ly*."

Nietzsche seeks self-overcoming, Kierkegaard infinite resignation.
Aeschylus could tell a tyrant from a turnip. Virgil, what the hell.

Our last leader emphasized my failings as a follower.

I would have waited there had I known then that I would see what I know now
I would have seen if I had stayed.

If I knew my visit's purpose I would know its length.

# Ice Bridge

24. And with *what* on their feet?

23. Always the old world we leave.

22. They made me wait. Apparently "life-threatening" admits of degree.

21. Out here, back then, you didn't chop enough wood for this winter, you got no chance to chop for next.

20. If you think polar means sealskin and albatross.

19. Disassociation, dese systolic rhydms, dat shepherd's pie.

18. Topiary yo mama. Topiary my ass.

17. I know you said "Te Deum," but I heard it as "tedium."

16. Winter here, colds coldern snow.

15. Sounded less like a bullet whizzing by than like a boy making bullet-whizzing-by sounds.

14. Had circumstances been otherwise. Had she been. Had I. God knows why she believed me for as long as she did.

13. No propane tanks inside. By order of the Fire Marshal.

12. Undone. U-N-D-O-N-E.

11. *They* didn't call it an ice bridge. Or have a concept of "continent." But nothing of theirs didn't fit on the sledge, Old Father could walk, and there might be seals.

10. In the note, though, he called the attack "viscous."

9. Heavy machinery, not today, not any more. A caution's a caution.

8. I know they migrate *now*, but what started them?

7. *That* cake eaten *and* haven.

6. Rheumatic undergarments, tubercular toys. Take me to your liter. Anything smells more like pigeons imploding onto wet cement than fatigue does, I'd like to know.

5. And a syntax that contested grammar.

4. Ever pheasant.

3. You got another thing comin.

2. Defy, define, definance. Deferential calculus.

1. NEVER would have stumbled those first steps upright, not if she'd foreseen THIS winter. Been just fine on all fours, hidden in the savannah grass.

# Dream Lullaby

*And there she lullèd me asleep / And there I dreamed...*

## Marie, Beside the River

Her name was Marie.  She had red hair.
This was long ago.  Now nothing's the same.
     Her name was Marie.  When they blew toward her,
leaves glided, graceful as birds.  And why not?
She had red hair that registered
how far we all are on our way to winter.
Teenage lovers gathered there
as if it were a park where they
could neck while others played guitar
or watched their dogs chase squirrels.
     This was long ago.  The part of me
she restored lived its moth-length life.
Happy people punted past,
one with sleeves rolled up to row,
the other to trail one arm the way
a drowsy willow trails its branches.
     She had red hair, she had long fingers.
She winced with each drag, but still I envied
her cigarettes those fingers, those lips.
She winced again when she exhaled.
She squinted in the river-bent light.
     Now nothing's the same.  Women bend down,
adjust the children in their strollers.
Laughter from couples at one with the current
competes with the clapping of pigeons scattering
from a man bracing his cane to stand.
To see her now, I have to squint.
     Her name was Marie.  She had red freckles.
Her hair when she lay back in grass
was thick enough to cover clover.
Retrievers, giddy in the river,
appeared as heads with wakes like wings.

This, all of this, was long ago:
the park, the river, the city, Marie,
her hair spread out across the grass,
the first leaves, the last clover.
The unsteady man leaving behind
a bench and bread crumbs and regathered birds.
Her cigarette held up to catch songs:
couples laughing through willow limbs,
dogs shaking off water, one
uncertain guitar, mothers humming
to soothe their children back to sleep.
    This one red hair was hers, is her.
Now nothing's Marie.  Her name is Long Ago.

# Dream Logic

*The language of waking life is always marked. In order to have real dreams, one has to sacrifice those marks — but this isn't to say that dreams don't love logic.*

I register here what fear erases.

    •

    •

Draw up what answer from what voice dropped down what mistrustful cistern?
Thin rope, tin bucket. Water solicits, assures; drought doesn't.
Even waterless, this water source offers condensation,
cold bucket. My voice called down into the ought-to-be-but-isn't,
yours echoed up. Consolation and quenching of thirst, sistren,
resist. Seldom are *both* offered us; I'd take either one.
The bucket's empty, but the rope still creaks to out-complain
the rust just where handle axles tin. Both whine, as hinges whine.

    •

What must words hoard, to cede clarity sufficient to pain?
To coo us thus so quietly through this too-loud world,
what patience must possess them, these paired doves, what mercy.
It's not true, I know, but I hold their hoots proof against pain.
Intonations could not, but trading them must, claim clarity
for salve, living (as we, too, live) at the mercy of this world.

    •

    •

    •

He takes careful notes, knowing objects sometimes stay obtuse.

    •

    •

Though I stop at nothing to know, I know it would not do
to know just anything, so though I claim no comprehension
I do propose — purport — particularity. *This* I know.
Not *there are spirits* but *I am haunted.* Not *there is return*
but *there* has been one. That she, the very who *never was* here,
*is* here. That I, who never was inhabited, now am.
That listening *for* is listening *to*; knowing another,
knowing otherwise. Not all ghosts at once, but one at a time.

    •

If this could continue, it could only as a letter
to who is no longer, about what never was, possible.
Dear Who Will Not Be Put To, I speak of What Has No, Use.
Am I sending you my thoughts when I send you this letter?
Or only giving myself reason to continue,
to put to use the put to use, make making possible?

          .

          .

          .

I understand love as a chair would understand a boat.

          .

          .

It seems to be in motion, this horizon, as do I.
But which motion causes which? Am I sick because my lurching —
me matching deck matching hull matching waves — troubles the sky,
or because the horizon's undulations are catching?
I thought I'd bought a ticket for the train, but even
where I speak the language I'm often ushered into lines
that head to destinations I didn't know I'd chosen.
Did I misspeak? Was I duped? To whom would I complain?

          .

How post my self in relation to something (anything)
beyond this uniform fencerow we misname *history*,
no post distinct from any other post not perched upon
by red-shouldered hawk or red-winged blackbird? If anything
were that evenly spaced, could anything else trace a self
except one chastened by, because wasted on, history?

          .

          .

          .

Better an arc subtend than that a segment bisect.

          .

          .

It swallows all it swallows, mass mistaken for mass,
swallows it all as storm surge swallows swaths of shoreline,
offers for the finding after only slivers of glass,
deflects off weathered edifice, trickles through tumbledown.
Deflects barely, a swallow off the surface of a farm pond.
Even on cold nights, not all brilliance mimics the crystalline.
Not all wisdom waits, not all that winters winters underground.
Unspoken, any summons to silent predation.

    •

I name it *Desolation Knob*, that ridge where wind and loss merge,
where what I see looks like something sight could not prove,
frost figured as so many bare branches.  And omens,
my god, so many, like animal tracks, but they merge,
blown over by another snow.  Body they once were, mind
they may since have melted into, omens may they prove.

    •

    •

    •

Moths gathered light to, and from, the streetlamp.

    •

    •

We waited at the edge for something else, something other
than this winter, so long we no longer know how to tell
what winter is, what name it answers to once become other
than itself.  So we called them snowfall, the moths, watched them swirl,
thought nothing of their not falling, since here, where we stood then
and stand still, snowfall *doesn't* fall, only swirls.  Like moths,
we say of the snow, as if we didn't know better when
we told the lie that they make honey of this light, these moths.

    •

As singing and knowing yourself no more than your singing
stand to one another, as strings' instructions resonate
through suggestible spruce, as your own voice, more felt than heard,
familiar less from the song itself than because you sing,
visits, but from inside, so must *your* song be what *they* know,
sung in a way that invites them, too, to resonate.

　　　　　•

　　　　　•

　　　　　•

Impossible to answer doesn't mean unfair to ask.

　　　　　•


　　　　　•

I've forgotten if I'm opening the shades or closing them.
The light outside won't say in this moment of eliding,
when all that is shone upon (and all *is* shone upon) seems
to do the shining.  Is this day beginning or ending?
Am I having trouble staying awake, or sleeping?  I've lost track
of which lost love I'm lamenting, which inevitable loss
you, love, defer.  Though, shone upon by this light, you do shine back.
Am I lost only here, or would I be lost anyplace?

　　　　　•

What if — why not — the geologic triad: heat, pressure, time?
If only for the period of the poison's passing through.
What region does the map presume to name, but not dare map?
As the bunting corrupts color, the pear perverts time.
Would it speak *of* but not *about* this terrain to name it *heat*,
this place we map by being lost in, by moving through?

　　　　　•

　　　　　•

　　　　　•

What do I feel like?

　　　　　•


　　　　　•

We need not close our eyes to know we're breathing, but it helps.
I feel now what escaped my feeling when I was feeling it.
Ours would be a bed, as ours is a love, of incipience.
I am *aware* of your breathing, though I am not hearing it
here, now, in this your absence, this best lost approximation
of silence the world has wistfulled us.  I know your body less
from the press of our embrace than from my imperfections,
from what I *do* feel when I feel neither my body nor yours.

　　　　　•

I could not, before you had, have guessed that you might yet,
or that after so long not, you would. You — *you*, the one who.
I know the others all, but never never would I myself.
Save for your declaration, I'd be heeding your warning yet,
though even when we could never, it seemed we always had.
Or maybe each of us makes the other a person who.

     •

     •

     •

What kind of cosmos must this cosmos be, to laugh at us like this?

     •

     •

Luck, to be luck, should last longer in fact than luck does. It *does*
look at you, not as a lover looks at you, all sorrow
and exile and incompletion and snowswirl, but as
an owl targets prey, sight more than sight, the seen seen through to,
the seer's sight no single sense but convergence of senses.
*That* makes luck luck, makes the lucky in love lucky not
for the love but for the luck, the being looked at as
luck looks at the victim its convergent senses target.

     •

Can my lucky love contradict love's contradiction?
Does luck possess her love, or replace it? *Instead of* spring
or *as* spring, the tulip? What distinguishes verge from cusp,
cusp from brink, musk from fetor, love from contradiction?
Does her warm surf and palm sway sway love to contradict
her snowmelt here in the mountains, at the cusp of spring?

     •

     •

     •

Dew litters this lawn with stars.

     •

     •

He prowls attics and landfills, where others' love letters land,
because no lover drops him letters for his own.  He addresses
long letters, longhand, to no particular beloved.
Nice paper.  Posts them to made-up names at made-up addresses,
because made-up is love, as if it were particular.
To each imagined recipient of each neat-margined note
he projects past the window he props open even in winter:
*What its gold eye sees, I see.  I sing the song in its glass throat.*

                    •

When I say *compromised*, I mean *intimate with others.*
I mean *Had we not spoken.  Were there some hope.  Yes,* that *gap.*
Until dandelions and bindweed crowd one another,
spring has lushed only the calendar.  To hear the others,
you'd think we were in love, but both of us intimate,
between what we show one another and how we are, a gap.

                    •

                    •

                    •

This makes more sense as an elegy than as a love poem.

                    •

                    •

My windows don't open.  They overlook the tarpapered roof
of a neighbor I infer from trash bags tumored by the door.
Minuscule fossils mar the roof's thinly scattered gravel, proof
of what?  Outside town, it's car tires that top all the trailers.
Silk peonies — really polyester — periscope from snow.
Peculiar intimacy, this: I couldn't call you by name
or pick you from a line for the police, but I know
your junk.  That '49 Ford, thistles wrestling rusted chrome.

                    •

All this you call collecting I call a taking stock:
no one thing sudden as a fall, but all a pull full forward
toward the overlook that overlooks the overlooked,
the Valley of Never Mind, the village Out of Stock.
They converge, caused and causing, collected and collecting:
as the sought-for fall back, the often-overlooked drift forward.

        •

        •

        •

You'll hear why I call it *Intimate Avalanche.*

        •

        •

He said as he opened his notebook. *She* said. *Her* notebooks.
And not hers except as something briefly, grudgingly loaned.
Crammed with loose sheets kidnapped from their sisters strewn across her desk.
Table, really. But overlooking the sea. The once sea, turned
desert. Turned ocean of scrub the color of the ocean.
Or whose color changes with the light as the ocean's does.
But with mountains for horizon. After a largo given
by solo oboe, a final movement enforced by full chorus.

        •

To remember (or, better, to re-experience as if
your last chance to refuse were your first to understand)
you must re-muster not events themselves but their contexts,
what does not present but does imply them, gives them *as if*
rather than *so help me God.* Only defeat can remember,
only collapse creates context enough to understand.

        •

        •

        •

He wonders now how his life will change.

        •

        •

Or that at least is what he tells himself he wonders,
though the telling himself so *means* he wonders how soon
he will see, and feel the consequences of, the ways
his life already *has* changed because of what happened.
What's done can't be undone, nor what follows from it known
or averted: when was that ever not our predicament?
He wishes he'd read more books in school, never moved to town,
known she was going to go before she went.

        •

To lend it leverage, teach it torque, I offered the machine
as I built it what blessings I knew: blessings for the air,
for gaskets and silicates, for the righting of things askew.
May its operator, too, offer blessings for the machine:
that it function with, and give, confidence, that as it torques
all else it torque itself askew enough to hum an air.

.

.

.

Maybe you know your way home, but I don't know mine.

.

.

I am become the silence I sought, but failed, to contain.
Not by ceasing speech, but by facing silence when I speak,
progressing toward it, addressing silence with the spoken.
Even when I sought it, what I sought was not what now I seek.
What is shelter, fully realized, if not imprisonment?
Imprisonment, if not shelter?  Thus my preference
for orientation over essence or achievement,
my failures to transmute refusal into defiance.

.

Is declination, cannot capture fragments fallen from.
Resolves into blue shimmer outside TV images in.
Grows more belligerent each time the necessary.
The image of the image of an image from.
Redefines as trust what is its failure to capture.
Is necessary to, but separate from, not inherent in.

.

.

.

Light within may insinuate, but does not derive from, light above.

.

.

The lights we're lit by, by those same lights are we seen.
Our shadows, agents of the lights' surveillance, follow us,
so many identical unbathed, underfed urchins.
If I can't shake them, does that mean my shadows *are* shadows,
or mean they are not? Why and how did it happen
that I have their share, but don't have it to give them? I profess
belief in burrowing, often imagine hibernation.
Though I could do neither, could never, still I'm envious.

                    •

My slow convalescence has been perforated by fear,
has known not *what* one, but only the fact *that* one, whispers.
Been withheld from the whisperer, given as itself only
to the whispered-to, who name it what it nourishes: fear,
expiration. Heard, in dreams their words perforate,
the radiant speak, but only to each other, in whispers.

                    •

                    •

                    •

As my losses accumulate, my modes of grief must morph.

                    •

                    •

Must turn to lingerings on patios as they, and thus
as I myself, sink beneath the sedimentary,
all those dusks silting all those seasons. Must mark all those
blossomfalls followed soon, even suddenly, by leafslurry.
Must measure my steps now because what these brownings-down
have done to unsettle the bricks also unsettles me.
Must resist this insistent listing toward caution,
this recession of sin toward impossibility.

                    •

They're colder, these older modes of mourning, than what they mourn.
They're braver, those who crest death silently, than we who weep.
To listen to wingflurry is to listen for names.
To gasp the ascent of the fretted flock is to mourn.
We secure a single register *when* we multiply modes,
we who have names, and give them, we who know we die, we who weep.

&bull;

&bull;

&bull;

One mode of enclosure works as well as another would.

&bull;

&bull;

Outlining in rowan leaves, festering with effervescents:
either keeps what was what it was from what is what it is.
I prefer the sort of proof that needs no evidence:
one's measure anticipating another's calibrations.
When have men (the gender of envy and impenitence)
not affected the infinitely foliate, not gone
disguised as feathered creatures, things pinnate, grassy places?
When have we not hunted together, and scavenged alone?

&bull;

The less informative information proves, the more forceful
its foregoneness, its being forced on experience
as if — because — first forced on carloads and categories.
My love, my fears, my wanderlust: which will prove most forceful?
Than her body, what registry archives more information?
After it, what categories could classify experience?

&bull;

&bull;

&bull;

Though none of us intended, we all of us chose, this ruin.

&bull;

&bull;

So many dominoed homes, animated then abandoned
by the what if not bewilderment, frantic in its flight.
So much always was fuel, as tepid now in its never mind
as it was hot in its got to right now right here tonight.
The better off for not knowing, consumed all the same.
The looked like it might last longer, the thought surely it would,
the not made to withstand such conditions, the only *seemed* calm.
The would have that outnumbers but still lost to what did.

&bull;

Those few who do escape do not escape unscathed.
*What* they escape when they escape is not harm, not mortality,
and there's no escaping past without brushing against.
Those from whom the escaped escape are not themselves unscathed.
Confined by their confining, they too pursue escape,
try to magic past, not brush against, their own mortality.

      •

      •

      •

I tell you this lie to avoid telling you a worse truth.

      •

      •

Rain mosses slate roofs, musks fallen leaves, mocks cigarette butts
arrayed at the curb. People poise newspapers uselessly
over their heads. People stoop as they step from shelter to bus,
they duck as if ducking would make the drops stop shoulder-high.
People make a choice this rain imposes: speak more loudly,
or more clearly, or not at all. A soaked mongrel
shivers. Her ribs reiterate the drain grate that sorts debris
by size. Under a back porch, black newsprint bleeds into black soil.

      •

Discarded because we wanted something worse, the detritus
of prior self-deceptions (plenty replaces neediness,
*this* love will last) accumulates. Phrases from old songs,
names loosed from faces. Faces themselves: detritus
from old friendships, other lives. Only as this now-discarded
could these the once-named sing our need as my neediness.

      •

      •

      •

In my nightmares, icebergs sheer from glaciers as ravens from bare trees.

      •

      •

There is no knowing that the postal carrier
didn't get the gate quite latched when she left the yard
after dropping off a box. No reason not to run upstairs
to change into shorts, it'll just take a second.
The baby just stopped crying, let him play. No way to recover
that moment between the perfectly familiar complaint
of the hinges and that sudden presentiment. It's over.
No catching him, no calling him back in time from the street.

     &bull;

Like footsteps, running, horses galloping — like gasping for breath.
Like the sting, in a cut or in your eyes, of perspiration.
Like a stubborn window that won't quite open, or quite close.
Like the rasping of wood against wood, imitating breath.
Like trouble chasing trouble past, trouble galloping
close enough to hear its breath, see its perspiration.

     &bull;

     &bull;

     &bull;

What began as mingle became bump up against.

     &bull;

     &bull;

Ellipses yearn toward circularity. As among us
who does not. Completion, invariance, infinitude.
Merely saying the words feels satisfying. But the ellipse:
*two* centers, *four* circles, overlapping just so. My god.
What something is need not *determine* in order to *bear on*
what it should be. Somewhere a universe compound
of circles spins, effortlessly. Against such perfection
I followed what I followed to find what I found.

     &bull;

Better one's own plain than others' complex ways-of-saying.
Better follow a wrong map than be the located-by.
Better worry than ease, better fretted-over than trusted-in.
Better give over than accept any said for its saying,
observed for enacted. Better point than line, line than plane,
plane than solid. Better caught-up-in than buoyed-along-by.

•

•

•

As if my wandering through darkness could lead others out of it.

•

•

We counted out in threes.  Not because the game demanded groups
or we were invited to play, or even because there was
a game for which any of us knew rules or purpose.
We must have made an even number; the counting always
came out wrong, no matter how often we repeated it.
Someone got left out; someone *had* to.  We kept counting, though,
because being counted meant we *could* play if a game *did* start.
Before the counting, I counted.  After the counting, no.

•

As if death, which should not, *did* resemble coming home from work
to a ransacked apartment.  Nothing missing, but things are
no longer yours.  They felt intimate once, but now they don't.
The wedding ring, post-divorce: same thing, just doesn't work
the way it did.  They had heft then, but here, so near my death,
names hollow out.  I don't know who I was, or who you are.

•

•

•

Late summer, we walked along the shore looking down at the moon.

•

•

"We" here means me and my memory of her as she was,
or as I had *thought* she was when I thought she loved me.
So often did she protest she loved me that even she must
have thought she did.  "Late summer" names that time, our time, only
as I remember it, not as it happened.  As I live
that time, now that I know my mistake, know that of course
*we* never happened, only wanted to, ought to have.
Had there *been* a shore, perhaps there could have been an us.

•

If not as lament, how engage these predilections
for solitude and silence and enclosure and distance?
I call them, as I call all else I long for, losses.
I learned this from her: my griefs *are* my predilections,
my joy *is* my self-destruction.  What else to lament
if not that I got the losses I wanted, and the distance?

     •

     •

     •

Here the weather threatens often, the landscape always.

     •

     •

Hills define this horizon.  Or we *call* them hills, because
*crags* would credit them, and we, stingy and foreshortened, fess
only crockets, only accidents and futile gestures.
*Monuments* would assert too much, would force us to curse
as more than shadow the looming of these loomings.  We hear
what we hear because they sing what they sing in small voices,
titmice and icemelt, beyond which none of us dare to dare,
voices whose ominousness we easily suppress.

     •

I thought I could turn, was turning, anger into music
(and who ought not make mathematical her malice?).
I thought I could command cancelling, extenuation.
I thought music mustered, I thought it *was*, more than music,
thought others awash in what I was awash in: anger,
exaggeration, extenuation, envy, and malice.

     •

     •

     •

Who drew you drew with one fine pen.

     •

     •

As appears in photographs, and *only* in photographs,
the only place you appear. Only snow registers
your footprints, not mud. I believe only your lies, not your truths,
though you lie badly, and I know the difference.
Their being *false* doesn't keep your lies from being *right*.
Your ribs fully tally grasses, as your fingers number stars.
No laws you follow follow from those that create me finite.
Your eyes are as full of the sky as the sky is.

     .

They contradict each other, my versions of our story.
I was all the witnesses to the accident, erasing
the event itself, deforming it into bent tellings,
all incompletenesses and partialities. Each story
by itself is whole, but together they contradict.
This the very telling of our story is an erasing.

     .

     .

     .

Pain pacing the second floor awakened pain on the first.

     .

     .

This hurt hurts like hushscuffled hardwood, that hurt hurts like snow.
These pains, patched, approximate patience, stitched into a quilt.
This grief performs the oceanic, rising up from below.
This loss registers as brittle skin to shed, plumage to molt.
Pain as the unity of owed and owed to. Pain as an owl
silhouetted at dusk. Pain in the forest grained the wood,
pain at night pocked the precarious moon. At what peril
does rain contest the rained-on, despair test weight that outweighs lead.

     .

To illustrate any speaker's inability to sing,
extend the sequence of her argument forever.
To grasp the impoverishment of mere particulars,
imagine melody careless of harmony's spacing.
To sacrifice order to direction, become that speaker.
Lose the particulars of *this* pleasure to some forever.

    •

    •

    •

If it *were* radiant, it would shine against such dusk as this.

    •

    •

Pale pink blossoms impertinent on the plum, apple trees
whiskered white. Or so the spindrift insisted, and the smell,
and the sizzle of hummingbirds and bees. This, despite chainsaws
at work half a mile off, the crack of a trunk surely a full
hundred years old, impenitent whoops from the boys.
Despite reminiscence of snow in the glow that time of day.
Reminiscence, or premonition. Despite all the noise.
Despite, or because of, my body's floating away.

    •

Escape disguises removal from place, family, home.
*It's right about* there. *Everything's fine here, how're things there?*
*They're hardly rolling hills, but people here call them mountains.*
*Again this year, she swore* this *would be her last visit home.*
Some said we wanted in spite, some because, of the removal
to return to the mountains. As if home had ever been there.

    •

    •

    •

The one warning is an animal odor on her tongue.

    •

    •

The rabbit, watching the bobcat, makes itself small and still.
When her fawn raises its head, ears high, so does the doe.
The school of herring, sensing the tuna, clusters and swirls.
The alert are not alert because they know, or want to know.
The absolute attention paid the world by prey species:
in us, poetry. I wish I had something else to report.
What do, what *could*, senses serve except vulnerabilities?
What is there but the inevitable, and the waiting for it?

    •

No hue outcolors color's absence, no movement outmoves stillness.
It has names, this urge toward where urgency begins,
this honoring of attention over result: privacy,
silence, ahimsa. Where conquest and commerce displace stillness,
the one repletion is emptiness, the one worth, absence:
privacy *of* privacy, the silence before silence begins.

      ·

      ·

      ·

Sure, the tide is low, but that doesn't mean it's not still dropping.

      ·

      ·

Curious what doesn't count as elevation, and what does.
Who gets to ascend, who must stay home and wait to hear.
Who gets praised for ascents made, who remains anonymous.
As if some were born for ticker tape, or because some are.
Elevation measures more than we admit it's measuring,
*assigns* more than it ought, such as who was born for burden.
Elevation compacts into one trespass all treachery.
It takes *pride* in how many more reach base camp than return.

      ·

In place of any apt conception of global extinctions,
our *forms*: skyscrapers, dams. Building which proves us present
not at all, only compromises our capaciousness,
defining creases to contain what must tear. One extinction
will be ours, but meanwhile those forms replace a conception
capacious enough to cross from past to present.

      ·

      ·

      ·

Time can reveal only what it has first obscured.

      ·

      ·

Did I become the registry, or was it already me?
Am I more fully myself with this identity
or no longer myself at all? Does *it* know *me*
when I know it? Does my knowing it *in* my body
give me to know it *as* my body? In the registry,
as the registry, am I the registered? Are they me?
Does *its* bring as consequence *my* approaching infinity?
Did I register myself, or did They register me?

                    •

To sway one's hips as one opens, is to open, a door.
One sways one's hips just the way the wind sways cedars.
One *wants* to wonder, Am I still on the trail? *Is* this a trail?
One incurs obligation to motion, passing through a door.
One loses one's own hips in another's hips
as one loses one's way losing a trail through old-growth cedars.

                    •

                    •

                    •

Even a wonder that already limps, logic yet will hobble.

                    •

                    •

Say I were harnessed to them, my failures.  Say when I lean
this far forward I would fall if not for makeshift tethers, taut.
If instead of *carrying* I *drag* it, is it a burden?
If in slowing me down it also holds me up?  Mustn't
I say the sledge does the carrying proper?  If snow outlines
the badly balanced boxes, separates them from the saggings
of these equally unsteady bundles, then what defines
the outsized sadnesses I've felt for so many so small things?

                    •

Given the system's tendency to translate background noise,
does the contest of dust and rumble with language
on this packed bus mean that, here, whatever's said, all saying
asserts itself as music?  Who could sleep in this noise?
When did my declaimings so decline that they merely translate
into one what I should be saying in another language?

    •

    •

    •

At first I didn't see the contours of the problem.

    •

    •

I hear voices when I'm halfway to sleep, and when
I'm half awake I hear them again. Which makes my sleep
not sleep at all, but measurement, in units of *between*.
Units of open window, units of decayed cassette tape.
Open, or *as if* open. As if played back dustyears later,
after the speakers have achieved, have *become*, patience.
As if *again* without first having been before.
As if *until* without a corresponding *once*.

    •

What else, narrowed, narrows the definition of torture?
How else than bunkers and lies protect what's here
from infection by what festers and putrefies there?
Not everything that looks like torture should be called torture.
Other freedoms sum to freedom of definition.
I'll see your *dark out there*, and raise you by this *dark in here*.

    •

    •

    •

What speaks heat must have been spoken by grit.

    •

    •

It inscribes as scrub the indifference to design
of Desiccation, the deity we desert indigenes
disdain (not all gods want praise) but still profess with cairn
and petroglyph. And attend as totem: the scorpion,
the elusive chaparral. Or this gila I happened across,
basking on blacktop. I threw a sweatshirt over him, tossed
him on the seat next to the six-pack, brought him back to my place.
We don't speak, but he seems at home, indifferent to thirst.

    •

Any ontology adequate to the body
would manifest not sequential process *to* an idea
but structuring that *is* idea, an architecture
that invites *return*, one body to another body,
the body to itself.  Any body's ontology
would first need architecture, to become idea.

     •

     •

     •

We stood in the stream as though risen from it.

     •

     •

Which of us remembers those skewed tunes the other's mother hummed
over the hemming she pretended between blowing her nose
into the crushed handkerchief and wiping her eyes, mascara thumbed
into smears?  Ours was no swan-graced stream whispered to by willows,
margined by meadows flush with clover, bee-lazy.  Not hardly.
It gave us to remember copperheads and rootballs, bald tires
and rust-festered turpentine tins.  We looked away mostly.
Still we saw plenty, a lifetime's worth for our hoarse nightmares.

     •

I stood my whole childhood by the neighbor boy, watching trash burn.
When since have I known all I needed to?  What childhood
wanted, it took so surely that each next taking loomed,
layers of haze over fields no one then bothered to burn.
Was it that blackened barrel, those two boys, or their watching
that loomed smoke-like over the choked-back hopes of my childhood?

     •

     •

     •

Who can tell too much attention from too little?

     •

     •

When the old couple's old Cadillac listed from its lane
into the median and flipped, plenty of other drivers
stopped to help, but what could they do? For a while, the woman
was conscious, but couldn't move, and no one could move her
because the doors were crushed closed. People called for help, of course,
but they were far from any town. The way she was pinned,
she could not see him. Just as well. Before she lost consciousness,
though, a woman reached through the broken windshield to hold her hand.

.

Combined with prayer or substituted for it, meditation
circumvents no suffering. How many mechanisms
do? Yet here we pose, eyes closed, monitoring our breathing.
To name what as *who* has marked us: is that meditation?
In forfeiting petition, we wished not to preclude prayer,
but to replace with quiet breathing noisy mechanisms.

.

.

.

I found our ruin beautiful even then, and find it beautiful still.

.

.

Where I may walk, when I should walk there. Into whom
I may convince myself the walking might make me. What,
of all that the walking only defers, I may assume
I have escaped, or will escape. How far to trust
those I have no choice but to trust, myself chief among them.
Toward what distinction I should pretend to progress.
The first decision should be the first decision. Come.
We will be taught trouble, have been so taught, have taught others.

.

The lists are enormous that progress from loss to loss.
The lists recount catastrophe, tally the terrible.
The lists prefer curse to prayer, defiant to reverent.
The lists list lessening, lusterlessness, loss, loss, loss.
The lists test fear against the long-shadowed Enormous.
The lists pledge to the reverent only the terrible.

    •

    •

    •

Sometimes I want what I want, but not often.

    •

    •

That trailer, tires on top, god knows why, who was I to ask.
I thought I was feeding the cats — the place simmered with strays —
until one night I forgot. Easy to do: double shifts, tasks
lifting and hauling, all in hot sun. I was young those days,
but it didn't help. A knock at the door woke me,
worried me, it wasn't like I knew my neighbors.
A raccoon. Waiting at the bowl, another three.
I'm not making this up. I put out food, of course.

    •

Who but the broken may break with the social order,
refuse imposed desires, eschew whatever's in demand
at the moment? What it might mean to be serious?
By breaking out of one to break with another order?
Alternativity as repair of the broken
by the broken, seriousness in place of demand.

    •

    •

    •

The world needs its pulse taken, that's for sure.

    •

    •

How far would you have to walk to find potable water?
If poetry has not been asking that question, why not?
Out here, whole towns, abandoned, have gone back to mule deer
and ptarmigan after generations of winter wheat.
How would you heat your home? How far *is* affluent from feral?
How suddenly would you have to leave? What would you bury?
Already above us — out *there* — satellites send signals
nothing here any longer receives. Strange times. I worry.

    •

Our divine natures and our animal simplicities
observe one another when no one is observing them.
Each finds in the other unaccountable comfort.
We should know to mistrust our animal simplicities
*before* we see them stalk and devour our grace-tinctured natures.
Still, it gives unaccountable comfort, this observing them.

> .
>
> .
>
> .

I find that their flyways account for my cravenness.

> .
>
> .

Honeysuckle suffocating twisted cedar trunks
still posted in rows, though what fencing once tensed them long since
fell away. Yellow-headed blackbird, western meadowlark,
yellow-breasted chat. For me, it gives release to leave sentence
for list. Wilson's warbler, goldfinch. To name, to believe.
How much more harried and brutal and brief could those lives be?
Yet, how much closer to the sun could anything live?
Toadflax, gumweed, western wallflower. Vetch, sage, snowberry.

> .

A life speaks time in one, but time speaks lives in various, ways.
Here I sit, on the surface of one of countless cysts
on this carbuncled cosmos, blemished with boils and bubbles.
Quantum retells the *Timaeus* in various ways.
They just add defects, my furious attempts to bind time
to my lives on the surface of bubbles, my lives inside cysts.

> .
>
> .
>
> .

This place: isolated, yes, peaceful, no.

> .
>
> .

I return because it was here I saw what I saw,
because when I return, though it has not, I *have* reverted.
I return for once-goldens, almost-glintings, nearly-birds, now
married to mud, no longer responding to wind, bruise-rotted.
I return for shagbark, serviceberry, shorewhisper, the drone
of frogboom and bonescatter, bleached crayfish claws, any kind
of unassimilated dialect. I return to rejoin
what one never leaves, all this process, steady as stargrind.

> •

It didn't *have* to feign bird call or mimic beetle click,
the soft slap-slap, in rhythm with his walking, of work gloves
in the back pocket of my father's jeans, applauding dust,
furrows plowed, hogs fed. *Shut up and do your chores, son.* Quiet click
closed of a gate well-repaired. What if not poetry to call
road dust, tools arranged just so in the shed, those work gloves?

> •

> •

> •

This landscape became *this* landscape by being first bent, then burnished.

> •

> •

Consider what principles this terrain reifies.
*Wear down*, for one, *as you have been worn down. Buckle and shift,*
for another. Who ever thought the land offered guides
for human conduct? Who thinks so now? It is not a thrift,
the land's accommodation. Nor is it an investment,
our irrigation. *Exile as you have been exiled*
being *our* principle. The land as enemy combatant
photographed for a keepsake, naked but for the leash we hold.

> •

Does closure do to the closed what renaming does to the named?
*Extraordinary rendition*, say. Those pivots
for *rs*, vowel-revolved. How someone's saying so magnifies
any said. Said, Ahmed, Khalid: these the *un*named.
Does the fact of our unnaming *them* draw any closer
the changes that *it*, reality, magnifies and pivots?

      •

      •

      •

*These* objects, no others.

      •

      •

The wardrobe my mother's father made for my mother's mother,
big as their caskets side by side, stood on end, and as heavy.
To make the shadow looming over my sleep feel familiar,
I ship the wardrobe — useless ballast — city to city
as I fail. Silver tarnishing in a cracking leather case.
Chipped china, surely lead-glazed. Grainy black-and-white candids
of relatives I never met and couldn't name. Placemats
crocheted by Aunt Absent to measure measureless solitude.

      •

From the brutality of brutal circumstances,
only brutality follows. Don't think that you
would not be brutal then, are not already. Don't think visions
will angel you, unanimal your circumstances.
Don't think you *will* think. That's one form it takes, brutality:
thinking the visions you are given are given *to you.*

      •

      •

      •

One person photographed photographing another.

      •

      •

Neither any longer fit subject for a photo taken
in such weather, so long ago. Could either be alive still?
Not likely. Yes, *they're* young, but the picture's not. Yes, *someone*
saved it, with these others, in this shoebox, lid illegible
under attic dust, mistrustful stepsister to snow.
But the shoebox outlasted everyone, those we see
in the photograph, the one who kept it, any who would know
their names. Is well on its way to outlasting me.

      •

36

Answering one would raise two more of the questions lurking here.
What *is* blizzard fog?  What else makes action and inaction
equally treacherous?  I saw movement, but I thought
I saw light.  I should pull over, but not now, not here.
It's so *quiet*, the threat of the sudden.  They're *cold*, these questions
that blur thought as snow blurs light, as photographs blur action.

> .
>
> .
>
> .

Not what I wander through, but my wanderings.

> .
>
> .

If my wanderings *arrive at*, do they *occur in*, rooms?
I myself bear death's tincture, exude its very attar.
Still, I post apotropaics.  On the sill, geraniums
in pots factory-turned but hand-painted with stylized figures.
Wind-worn sandstone for a doorstop.  Books, not because their wisdom
protects, but because alphabetizing them does.  No lid
on the jar that collects coins and useless keys, brings sea glass home,
not in colors water does show but in those I wish it did.

> .

All this rattling of these my unrests tests me, proves me tin.
It insists on arguing for segments, against the line,
for jaggedness, against direction and the metrical.
Sporadic clattering hammers my image into tin,
makes me my own best guess at chaos, catches me rattling
after the anti-metrical, fragment rather than line.

> .
>
> .
>
> .

I would trust the map more if I trusted the terrain less.

> .
>
> .

Storm swarms in from the west, frenzies the wheat. Shivers knick-knacks
from shelves onto the shag. This tenuously tied-down trailer
will buckle in some funnel soon, but while you relax,
secure on your foundation, I *feel* things. You should *hear*
these windows rattle. My rent is twice what this tinderbox
is worth, but half a shambles in town. Better
a hundred miles from the horizon than three blocks
from the market. There's such a thing as honest weather.

      •

If measurement or meaning could occur apart from context,
I would accept as context the context you supply, but
that chill wind blowing in off the bay has history
and nature on its side. As does fog, which turns any context
on its side. If all that *ought to* really *did* occur,
I'd accept, instead of measurement or meaning, history. But.

      •

      •

      •

We don't get to choose what we remember.

      •

      •

Answer me this: why *shoes* so often in the rubble?
How can the same force that separates them from feet
preserve shoes intact? Is it the troubled or the trouble
that ruins archive? Is ruin what we wait for or how we wait?
If I'd known the word at that age, I could have asked,
while he was there to ask, *Daddy, what caused your ruination?*
And, if I'd known the question (or sensed how soon the *at last*
of ruin's coming would come), asked also, *What will cause my own?*

      •

Who sings what to whom when music circumscribes the space
my own limits limit with, limit as, a circle
(calculation, name, to post in place of the outermost
outermost, measure and trope to substitute for space)?
When am I not erased, given over, given to music
that marks the circularity of the outermost circle?

    •

    •

    •

I move through space as others move, am moved by them.

    •

    •

Invented in every war by the occupied,
there is a hiding beyond hiding, intricate networks
of tunnels the invader knows of but cannot find,
a code women create to share crusts of truth, spread alerts.
Soon the invaders see enemies where there are none.
They call these elusive enemies first ghosts, then devils.
They fear, more than the real, these enemies they imagine,
that animate, in alleys or underbrush, their own troubles.

    •

Safety moves to the edges of any situation
once we start singing. It's not the one who *works*
with whom we fall in love, not the one we understand.
It was compromised already, our situation.
That's what we sing about when we sing. No safety
can give us to understand any least of how this world works.

    •

    •

    •

Before others could destroy us, we destroyed ourselves.

    •

    •

We have heard screams. At certain hours any silhouettes cast
against our windows should be cats, should not be cast by headlights.
We have heard screams, *and* how swiftly they are silenced.
Reports are sharper here, in the zone of shot-out streetlights.
We who heard screams made the one choice that was a choice for us,
to issue the reports, to be *behind* the headlights,
not outlined and blinded by them. We who heard screams gave ourselves
to anything we thought might substitute for streetlights.

    •

More often in institutionalized than in nuanced ways,
we learn to see ourselves as others perceive us.
Often what we see as ourselves when we see ourselves
as seen is the seeing in institutionalized ways.
Seldom does defeat arrive in bullets, often in
our acquiescing to see ourselves as others perceive us.

&bull;

&bull;

&bull;

Their opaque tears remain plainly visible under their transparent skin.

&bull;

&bull;

No more what if Security calls for corpses.
I commit here to that yet-but-rumored Clarity
in the flashing of which across an otherwise
dimly constellated All Disappears Into will be
ciphered the pledge of the Pledge to replace the Waits For All
with the Only For Us that will chase into shadow
the Shadowy. I will answer the call of the Call,
know what the Knowing, luminous as the Luminous, know.

&bull;

Toward peace, any angle bisects illusion.
Putti purport *lasting, perpetual* even, yet...
Yet. Point me to a pact other than hesitantly
consented to, a confirmation other than illusion.
Into relief and illusion, peace could not angle
more hesitantly than this. I trust the tentative. And yet.

&bull;

&bull;

&bull;

Any plea I made for help would only prove no one can help me.

&bull;

&bull;

If this my desolation had a name, what would name it?
Not the lisp against leaves of half-hearted high-desert rain.
(It's light here even when it's dark, dry even when it's wet.)
Not the owl commiserating with another distant train.
Does my sleeplessness mark this early morning or late night?
That shadow scratching at the compost, in different weather
will be stealing vegetables. (*You* try to be quiet
at this hour, in this place.) I won't be sleeping then, either.

·

The more willingly I accept how perplexing life is,
the greater the tension between a thing and its context.
That plastic cow I dug up from the garden: what's it doing
on this kitchen sill? The boy who lost it, who knows where he is.
Who knows if he finds his life, as I find mine, perplexing:
ever more routine events, ever less familiar context.

·

·

·

My soul may yet ascend as smoke; meanwhile my body burns.

·

·

Not with pine's fury, but inexorably, patient as peat.
My body does not argue with its skittish shadows,
outsized and invertebrate against the wall opposite.
My shadows do not argue against my prodigal ghost,
any more than it protests the one season this place hosts,
wind forever bearing into exile a crippled light.
Poor shadows, cast just here, cast for a century at most,
forever expecting some writ to commute their confinement.

·

Symptoms of the absolute as it relapses into time,
the marsh grasses mat, leave no surface to the waters.
Texture matches timbre in these leaves browned down in masses.
Passing clouds mirrored on water's surface only *measure* time;
water spared surface *becomes* it. Grasses enforce the absolute:
as hosts they rise from what as masses they impose on waters.

.

.

.

Even this long afterward, the falling continues inside me.

.

.

Not sequentially, many of me falling one by one,
each once and briefly, that's-thatted toward those previously,
but with similar suddenness and finality, fallen.
Not events, but a condition. Even for those of me
who are falling yet, the recognition that we must fall
creates a falling before the falling, anticipation
through which we fall into falling, the *but soon will*
that follows any *has not yet*. Fall, falling, fallen.

.

Once worlds have multiplied, nothing can remain quite
exclusive to any one. Nor is any one world
isolated or distinct. A hallucinatory
quality follows, any one world made unquiet,
animated by others, given by this, the multiplied,
hallucinatory energies that haunt this world.

.

.

.

My motions all shadow some larger motion.

.

.

As if within myself I bore from source to surcease
instructions for my own death, in script I cannot recognize
as script, much less read. Bellerophon. Carrier of the curse.
Uriah. Virulence itself, not just the virus.
What makes darkness, not what darkness makes, shadow and blight.
My movements mimic its movements, with mirror symmetry.
It advances toward Advance, I retreat from Retreat.
It moves toward the center of the Center. I move away.

.

The role of the serial in constructing the constructions
that order the disorder our griefs grieve deserves a whole
row of brittle tomes. Thanks to it, the rapidly additive
receives schema, becomes project not favela. Constrictions
of architecture replace restrictions of law, two roles
for the additive, each impersonating the whole.

.

.

.

When you touched me with something feather, I felt something husk.

.

.

Once boundless, always boundless, but it's not the saltscrabble crust
crunching underfoot, not the fish schooled here as fossils
in sediment rather than current, not the infinite west
in place of a horizon, but those wind-hecklers, the gulls,
that prove this desiccated place was once a sea.
Scavengers survive here by eating other scavengers.
This is the domain of buzzard and ant, crow and coyote.
Here, while one ribcage bleaches and dries, another scatters.

.

You are to me not numbers but what numbers substitute for:
the effects of gravity, all the permutations
of a leafpile. A thousand thousand, and counting.
You would be all increase, if increase could substitute for
what can be nothing but itself. You are of numbers
not their counting but their countless permutations.

.

.

.

But it's not their *names* these flowers whisper to me when I kneel to them.

.

.

Did what almost happened almost happen?  Did she not say
what I think she did not say?  Are there varieties
and degrees of impossibility?  Was it only
what I didn't hear that I forgot?  Did I forget *because*
I didn't hear?  Did I start to forget just after
she didn't speak, or just before?  History and botany
concur: I'm lost.  Now is not then, but will be.  I wish I were
more certain *in*, but less certain *of*, my uncertainty.

     •

Always arrive early at what arrives late to itself.
Always set aside something, or someone, to desire
in secret.  Better to lie about lust than memory.
Better than merely to mistake is to mistrust oneself.
I learn late, but may learn yet that I lie to myself always,
*must* lie, must misremember as one some other desire.

     •

     •

     •

I never guessed it would be this long before I *felt* anything.

     •

     •

Holding on to *what*?  Holding on *how*?  And for what purpose?
Held up to what misguided standards?  Believed on what grounds?
In defiance of what elaborate patiences?
What does mixture oblige that purity confounds?
Bulbs in a rock garden, what was he thinking?  But their texture
and patina yesterday when I sang them, mummies,
from that sand, reburied them not to rebirth but as gesture,
proper earth as lamentation.  Not *until*, but *because*.

     •

No knowing which parts of ourselves will go missing,
no kissing them goodbye when their going only shows us
their prior absence, the falseness of our histories,
shows us how like transparence to glass we are, missing
by definition, all wholeness loss, summed from missing parts,
absent from the histories that themselves are lost to us.

.

.

.

I have reason for being so unreasonable.

.

.

I mimic insects, affect the fungal and the igneous.
It's not my bites and burrowings-into that should worry you,
but their aftereffects, which may include dizziness,
metamorphosis, visits from mythic monsters, piercings-through
of the membrane containing you from dreams.  Perforation
only proves prior perforation, confirms the utterness
of loss in any having-lost, removes affectation
from the baitings of the never-to-be-borne-across.

.

If I believed in progress, I could believe things happen,
could release the quest, embrace the drift into apocalypse,
the cataclysm toward which our effortless, soothing
wanderings inevitably tend.  Things that happen happen,
as do things that don't, and things that shouldn't.  Progress
would welcome, even find soothing, any apocalypse.

.

.

.

In plotting a course for us, I claim cartographic license.

.

.

I mean to mean the map differently than do others.
Not by drawing it to an unusual scale, but by
drawing it otherwise, withholding scale altogether.
I say we *see* when we see that other standards apply.
I say we *arrive* not at landmark but at occasion.
A map need not be topical.  It might identify
events instead of landmarks: As Birds Convene, rather than
Pretension Peak.  Why *walk to see*?  Why not *be visited by*?

.

About our damage, the damage we do to each other:
it doesn't help to call it something else if it's damage.
About what, when we do it, we protest is not damage:
damage doesn't stop being damage to each other
by being damage to what else.  Other damage is damage
*because of* our damage, not *despite* our damage.

    &bull;

    &bull;

    &bull;

If this were an island we would speak frequently of fish.

    &bull;

    &bull;

One of us would have crossed the stone floor at first light
to open the shutters, knowing nothing about the weather.
Though the stones' dampness would tell us something, we wouldn't know what.
(We lack the sense cats and sparrows have that warns of a tremor,
the sense for which our incessant chatter cannot substitute.)
We would insist that if we knew its code of cloud and color,
the sky here could be seen to semaphore any secret.
We would take any giving up as a giving over.

    &bull;

My meanings I change whole, my sentences one word at a time.
You think I'm exaggerating, but I'm serious.
The language doesn't ask if you *like* the game it's playing,
doesn't offer transformation except one word at a time,
new vision or new life except as new sentences.
Playing at it does not make substitution less serious.

    &bull;

    &bull;

    &bull;

We both know empty spaces are never empty.

    &bull;

    &bull;

I set out on foot, before dawn, congratulating myself
with familiar incantations: moonlight, dew, birdcalls.
Goodwill inattentive to consequence: what else
to call taking as an invitation that line of hills
defined by anticipatory light as other than
what wants claim? What I want is to know how to resist.
How, inhabiting one place, to occupy none.
How to enact not the best intentions but the fewest.

·

Some remnant of the E nearest middle C, still sounding
in my mind after dying away in the air, calling
me from my desperate to its patient disappearing,
asserts its preference for dispersal over sounding,
invites me to fray, to turn similarly remnant.
Calls my disappearance to disappear into its calling.

·

·

·

Not some high thing but height itself stares down at you.

·

·

Absence itself shows through, not one of our substitutes:
the aura that is not dawn but announces dawn with light
that is not light but gives way to light, a cold past all colds past.
Not our common protestations: *Speak for yourself. Leave me out
of this. I trusted you.* In our eyes everything projects
inverted. What pinhole, what chiasmus, can govern
such inversion? Is it the backwards or the sideways that awaits?
What has been inverted when an absence appears upside-down?

·

I sometimes touch it, whatever it is, but I never know
whether, at a given moment, it, the mysterious,
massive something that withholds all familiarity,
is touching me. How would its touch feel? What would one know
who *did* know its touch? Any touch whispers of, but is not quite,
familiarity. Whispers mystery to the mysterious.

       •

       •

       •

Sounds like a trick question.

       •

       •

I *felt* it first, before I *saw* anything.  Felt it
as contrast to, absence of, footsteps.  Felt it as one feels heat.
Strange to hear stealth more insistently than assertion.  Strange that
I could see the fire but not the eyes, hear the stillness but not
what was still, sense the staring but not detect the staring one.
Strange that I could recognize, but not identify, danger.
Strange that I stayed there without *deciding* not to run.
Strange how suffused with curiosity was my fear.

       •

I loved there what could be loved *only* there.  I found the forest
effortless, mistook its stirred canopy for what abated,
not what communicated, atmospheric furies.  Hunger
*sang* to me there.  In place of shouting, leaf-stir.  The forest,
all owl-call, protested nothing, ate everything it loved,
loved not having but *being* the hunger nothing abated.

       •

       •

       •

I come to you from an expanse, overcast and lusterlorn.

       •

       •

This pattern of shadows matches neither the outlines
that challenge light nor the texture of the receiving surface.
This light source imposes shadows, but the contours
onto which they are cast obstruct even as they embrace.
Even the shadows of glass were visible to me then.
Can a shape *be* a shape other than the shape it *has*?
Is casting shadows a form of illumination?
My illumination then was shadowed absences.

       •

Of the unnoticed, things afforded no acts of attention.
Of things uncalculated as constituents of thought.
Of the one grief and its limitless extensions:
a lone tree, its roots assessing the whole field. Of attention
willed from underneath to under underneath. Of unnoticed
extensions-into and spreadings-across. Of littered thought.

    •

    •

    •

Consequence only *looks* fragile.

    •

    •

Subject thus to insistences and constancies,
he imagines as archipelago all his selves:
defined by wind and tide, populated by species
evolved without predators but extincted by invasives,
sheaved by the song, if song it be, of the dark-faced ground tyrant.
Everything translated, trinkets into tributaries.
Often mapped, seldom chronicled. In him, fulfillment and want
match. Butterflies and bats to pollinate the plants, but no bees.

    •

My charge: invent new ways, by building new spaces, in which
to question. Other curiosities. I resolve
against the catechismic, the interrogational, the meant
and believed in and insisted upon, the *for which
it stands* and *in which we trust.* I embrace — I add to — the ways
any resolution resolves more than it meant to resolve.

    •

    •

    •

I tell this story to highlight the importance of another.

    •

    •

What one painter would reduce to a few lines, an abstraction,
another would see as already thus reduced.
I keep *adding*, as if details could sum to intuition,
as if to locate the one truth that arranges all the rest.
I keep thinking if I only pay enough attention...
I keep thinking if I just keep thinking I'll discover
the almost hidden almost hiding in the almost hidden,
the whole that no accumulation of detail could offer.

·

When I stepped back in an attempt to see what I had done,
I saw I had done nothing but step back. My words evoke
more words. The places I have seen are names, not places.
When I step back I see as nothing my coming undone.
I see I can name nothing but what's been taken back:
I see I see places only as the losses they evoke.

# Dream Lexicon

*... all that we call lives and souls, lie dreaming, dreaming, still ...*

I would not ask you to believe my report that I found this as a yellowed sheaf in my attic (I don't believe it myself), so let me assert instead that this dictionary was dictated to me during a reverie, one of the spells to which in my steady declination I am prone.

Parts of speech, indicated in each entry by one of the following abbreviations, are speculative, since (a) the categories appear to be less discrete and more ambiguous than their closest equivalents (noun, verb, etc.) in waking languages, and (b) scholars' understanding of the grammar is incomplete.

    t. = timetable
    t. = token
    t. = transaction
    t. = trouble
    t. = turnstile


1. **spile** t. sturdy enough to lean against when gazing out to sea,
fugitive enough to die back in drought.


2. **grapnel** t. stream beds for logsink turning stone, shallow sea for bonesettle become not stone itself but shadows in it.


3. **toper** t. because even the arrantest may flag and, flagging, want
a two-penny friend to rouse him again.


4. **slippering** t. subtle gradations from random cuff through stiff stateroom check, from levelling to shock and awe to the formal.


5. **bosky** t. browned and brawny, unbecomingly bushy-bearded, bristly
but beloved, obeyed, unbuttoned, believed.

6. **superinduced** t. the others all protested sadness for the sisters despite their feeling none such for themselves.

7. **brevet** t. this boss became a boss by being obedient, that boss by being the biggest burro.

8. **cenotaph** t. who knows how many generations as *their* old home place, now someone else's old home place instead.

9. **obliquity** t. not the cause of visceroptotis, but one effect over which no herb, no nostrum, holds influence.

10. **salam** t. cheered by so cordial a chat, instead of straightway home I ventured the climb up Conspicuous.

11. **tester** t. not any undulation would, but this one undulation did, restore to her what fringed and fluted whatnots.

12. **vitiated** t. who last had her blood let, what doctor last performed a letting, who used the basin later, and for what?

13. **aye** t. there let it lie for ever and for, our love will last for, whose fragrant flowings-forth are infinite and.

14. **quohog** t. like any liberation else, this letting language loose proves itself easier said than done.

15. **comb** t. what may any wave claim beyond place in some larger washing, what use could cotton, not drawn off the cards?

16. **stiver** t. rather more than our penny, less than their pound, insufficient to stand for a pint or sum to a noble.

17. **pilau** t. from garrulous officer to sullen chief of police, from cedar shavings to truffles and grouse.

18. **drab coat** t. broad-skirted, unevenly hemmed, unleavened, level-headed, too swift, even leisurely, to estimate.

19. **confluent** t. as compared to her come-hither, consider his anterior hypapophysis and its strange centrum.

20. **costermongers** t. how if not through audience, before whom if not Justice, to what end except to settle accounts?

21. **scuttle** t. in a precipitate and most undignified manner; corn, grain, dust, manure, coals, water, more coals.

22. **marquee** t. not suffered by any self-respecting first officer, never pitched except in summer, and in port.

23. **succor** t. from impotent reason have we petitioners been cast, bereft, to wander brokenhearted away.

24. **puissant** t. how comes all this to naught, this naught, if there be something;
how comes all this to be if there be naught?


25. **quoggy** t. incommodious season to plow, incommodious place,
insatiable hunger, house all shambles.


26. **swart** t. pale pearl, smaller, smoother, smothered under sweeter tinctures,
given over to some huskier lover.


27. **craven** t. here: *sing* an indifferent air *with* an indifferent air
*in* the indifferent air: there.


28. **abandonedly** t. as it is well from time to time to improvise shelter,
so too from time to time is it well to wander.


29. **tow** t. before it is heckled, before it is scutched or soaked or worked,
before it is let go, before let go of.


30. **binnacle** t. on the weather side of, in the lengthening shadow of,
on the deck of, near the very one with which.


31. **phiz** t. less sensible and steady than freckled and intransigent,
more of another than of this world.


32. **physeter** t. by withdrawing any air from, owing to the pressure of,
forced through *by*, forced through *to*, vaguely known as.

33. **hustings** t. the one who must beg to be admitted to must beg to the one a table is provided for.


34. **menial** t. continuance of years having adjoined divine instincts to this mortal casing by menial strings.


35. **carking** t. et up she was, et up with care and curvature, all et up with penury and slander and mistrust.


36. **razee** t. how different (to what degree) and *how* different (by what means) is a half-enslaved mind from one enslaved?


37. **pommel** t. we chiromancers call this part the punch or the percussion, because it tells us what we know already.


38. **insult** t. Dody Stickle down the street ate paste, drank ink from ballpoints, until her parents took her out of school.


39. **solus** t. that sweetest, most amorous song, always sung, alas, before a painted backdrop, to an empty stage.


40. **chassee** t. how much lead in how much paint eaten by how many children in how many gutterfallen duplexes.


41. **fell** t. others slogged slowly through sludge to make their way down, but I passed, clinging to the neck of the bareback Devil.

42. **howdah** t. caparisoned in crimson, panoplied in purple,
ermined, arrayed in pompous regalia.


43. **butt** t. sole, fluke, plaice, turbot, mackerel, schulle, thornebake, halibut:
what species slicked the amazed disciples' ankles?


44. **devious** t. said of certain circumnavigations, suited also
to the spreading of a wave-vexed slick.


45. **thwack** t. such sanctuary as we despairing may devise of shruff,
moss, and hair, the stuff loss offers care.


46. **savage** t. for whom his numerous moan, for whom his very suspirance,
the breath of his breath, for whom the jointure.


47. **marline** t. in such particulars as pinfeather, in proportion
and appurtenance, in brief afterflash.


48. **sheaves** t. being bound as it rises does not preclude breaking apart
at its apex, dispersing like perseids.


49. **king-post** t. still approximate to permanence, even trussed, mortised, braced,
buttressed, coped, corbelled, lintelled, latticed, stayed.


50. **thole-pin** t. that midday heat concentrating concentrated heat: to touch
what we touched scorched and scarred our scorched, scarred hands.

51. **royals** t. all such mines of any such ore, all mulcts for all offenses,
all titles, taxes, revenues, and tithes.


52. **whelmed** t. how different is the guilt-given from the given-by-grace,
how different even is the giving?


53. **gam** t. most commonly on cruising-ground, oftenest in fine weather,
only infrequently in chop or surge.


54. **chicha** t. unforgivable to refuse, impertinent to decline,
impolite even to receive modestly.


55. **quarto** t. often issued to an indifferent, incurious world,
but seldom so sent forth unintroduced.


56. **hove-to** t. as cattle from too much too-moist clover, as turnips in sog,
so she of what must soon and suddenly.


57. **kedger** t. this bright basin, beaten from the singingest copper sheet,
bore libations to and oracles from.


58. **brit** t. the vertical cliff-face astir with predators frenzied
for what stirs in the horizontal sea.


59. **billows** t. still true, all I could not say to you I could not say it to,
until the ptarmigan trembles from the cold.

60. **reeve** t. one may stay above to charge others into hard confinement; one must go below to enforce the charge.

61. **piggin** t. for what higher aim would I want wealth than for a boy ever near to hold things fitting my necessity?

62. **disrated** t. if not lodged between voyages in a port plaited with plague, then at sea in a yellow-fever ship.

63. **curvetting** t. she did not, as she passed by, say what another might have said: fury may induce speed, but so may grace.

64. **shindy** t. though elsespeak offer it polite denomination and proper, yet may it bear but crude in downright dream.

65. **indite** t. so many so tidy markers in so many so long rows remembering so many so forgotten.

66. **a'lee** t. such a sea as never was broke open all it broke upon, splintering all ships it did not simply sink.

67. **heaver** t. unornamented, employed as a lever or purchase, able to lift what lifted gives relief.

68. **isinglass** t. steep two hours in stock seasoned to taste, transfer to skillet, sear for several seconds, garnish, and serve.

69. **rood** t. no square foot of surface stirred by sharks not sistered overhead
by stacked cubic feet aglimmer with gulls.

70. **maw** t. in token, this ring set with chalcedony, swallow-stones
I myself cut from the crop of one fallen.

71. **togged** t. long- and gnostically-knickered, supple as his nacreous saddle,
astraddle his sixteen-hand nickering bay.

72. **calomel** t. dulcis, further sublimated, a fourth time and upwards,
unto utmost dulcissimysticism.

73. **gamboge** t. one a bright yellow inclining to lacquer red, the other
dark urushi red dissolving to black.

74. **subtilize** t. rarify, mingle, refine, exchange, redistribute, reduce,
sublimate, extenuate, mysticize.

75. **scimetar** t. its voice, more sable than its feathers, fills the half-mile hills
and spills halfway across Fearful Valley.

76. **bethink** t. against all wisdom, and with all insistence, he assumed
the basest, the most poorest shape of all.

77. **pelisse** t. crimson velvet, ivory lace, hair she ever tries to tidy
against its own innate immodesty.

78. **far** t. esperant, aspirant, indicative, indexical,
illiberal, illegible, illicit.


79. **crescentic** t. behold the hemi-horizon, mark of genius, defect
abscessed across the forehead of the perfect.


80. **superincumbent** t. striations separating into fractures below but mounting
into a mantle of copsewood above.


81. **habergeon** t. they still cling to trees, those husks, long after their cicada souls
have returned underground, and they still *sing*.


82. **ancientest** t. the wisdom of, the reverend simplicity of, the seal of,
the writings of, the virtues of, the weight of.


83. **worsted** t. the said mystery and the sad misery and suffering sum
to soullessness: semblance sans semblance of.


84. **spigot** t. a man with a mallet making measured movements against oak
to give discreet vent to the vintage within.


85. **irradiate** t. midnight lightning may leave first a briefly lingering afterglow
but finally imposes darkness more absolute.


86. **direful** t. what do our times teach, if not the need for fewer convictions,
and far less earnestness in carrying them out?

87. **proa** t. all boats but the one commandeered, all women and children coerced to board, all reason set to sea.

88. **bashaw** t. down here we call em mud cats, and you aint noodled nuthin till you've had an arm in one up to your elbow.

89. **pandect** t. mark how little justice these our legislations effect, measure how much disgrace they disguise.

90. **ordinary** t. shall be elected by the citizens qualified to vote, shall preside over all sundry residents.

91. **attar** t. myself am the metope memorializing miseries, am the very congress of sufferings.

92. **pomatum** t. as restorative for her burned skin, I have mixed an ointment of apple pulp and bacon fat and bourbon.

93. **execrations** t. thei sworen, grete in voice, tempests of derision and contempt: *Mr. Fuckin Howdy Doody, Fly-Boy.*

94. **tendinous** t. taken from the tapering part, but with nothing to it to tempt, no least taste, no tenderness.

95. **mincer** t. all this, by simplest means: a series of cylinders, each scored end to end with parallel tapering grooves.

96. **batten** t. three inches broad, and two thick; five feet long, and four wide;
two feet from the ceiling, one from the floor.


97. **unvitiated** t. incapable of contrivance, constant in its increase,
with a crystalline logic all its own.


98. **shift** t. now must I dodge and palter, prey to all impress of power,
each least caprice of these unprincipled.


99. **moidore** t. to dispose of to ladies I carry one milled dollar, two doubloons,
a half Johannes, and this Four Pistol piece.


100. **surcoat** t. the whole college of heralds and half-wits caparisoned,
as if on horseback, or themselves horses.


101. **scrimp** t. any compensation possible, what alterations we can,
all accommodations necessary.


102. **vertu** t. to which we sacrifice the genuine pleasures of the soul,
to which we forfeit all for folderol.


103. **invested** t. unto which, having fetched her up by first light, they gave such chase
as could be called, were it possible, *patient*.


104. **chirography** t. conflicting testimony among experts in which reveals
its complexity and their simplicity.

105. **pods** t. some isolated populations have a less ochreous hue
and bear distinctive stippling and stigmata.


106. **potentates** t. none more pretentious, none more preoccupied with prestige,
none more pious, none more perfidious.


107. **belaying** t. the ingrossings, the circumventions, the manipulations,
the insults to parity or justice.


108. **dinning** t. done denying, done defending, done detailing, done with despair,
done with the dole, done done done with detox.


109. **burtons** t. two movable and one fixed, the two of darker hue than the one,
each given by each proper company.


110. **puncheon** t. what would be hardened by the fire must first by it be softened,
or so we say, having heard it often said.


111. **moles** t. not all the star-stirred waters in the immeasurable main
can wash away the mark you made on me.


112. **compunction** t. not all the marks you made on me together can corrupt
the constellations floating on these waters.


113. **gaff** t. if I am not the penny-paying public, I am *of* them;
with them, not with the dollar-drones, is my lot cast.

114. **abated** t. I would, except for this incessant hissing in my ears, these empty spots that rove across my vision.

115. **hilarious** t. among all who, against the wishes of the very ones who, sent to the same who, embraced by those who.

116. **imminglings** t. immaterialities, immelodiousnesses, immensities, immeasurabilities.

117. **asphaltites** t. unforgiven ghosts hover and float not for lack of bodies but because beneath them is not soil but pitch.

118. **dead-reckoning** t. when we say *haled home* we mean *gone missing*; by *streets of gold* we mean *I can't accept that I am next.*

119. **supernal** t. though I cannot, *because* I cannot, cross the space between us, I send these messengers to murmur grace.

120. **scud** t. the storm before the storm, that stirred its yeast of stubble and straw, the wind that warned of wind, then soon *was* that wind.

121. **lucifers** t. unwilling to forfeit themselves to plenty, they assumed deprivation, but brought with them very light.

122. **lashings** t. and trammings of broken rock, broken by those it breaks, borne on otherwise rust, these rails worn bright.

123. **quadrant** t. indiction, lustrum, season, momentum, uncia, atom: always toward indivisibility.

124. **tandem** t. both of us labored to load the logs, so both of us sat on the last for rest as we rode to the boom.

125. **spindle** t. this from Plato: all turns that must turn, and all must turn, spun into tunefulness on Necessity's legs.

126. **cunning** t. last in the list of illiberalities, but first to twist away from temperance and truthfulness.

127. **ferrule** t. all poles on which are displayed the standards to be at the least twelve feet in length, all barrels for vintage six round.

128. **conjure** t. nothing occurs uncaused, so there must be a miscreant, and miscreants must be caught out and cast out.

129. **hist** t. I began wonderful strangely to quiver and tremble and gasp, so afeared was I of headlong ruin.

130. **Parsee** t. neither burn nor inter your dead, but offer them instead to curs and other ravenous scavengers.

131. **shears** t. I hear from here the whetstone yonder whine, I hear wool rub against wool, feel the cool lanolin.

132. **innocency** t. lest I seem to have aught neglected in full defense of mine, lest in fact I neglect aught of hers.


133. **enticings** t. the shorter list, from then at least, would be of what was not an; for the longer list of, substitute her name.


134. **alow** t. I like aloft better, or am assured I should, and protest I do, though I mistrust myself, and she me.


135. **bitterer** t. can one of us be more, might I of all be most, comfortless, if we be equally unconfessed?

# Dream Longing

*Though we dream and hardly know it, longing, like an angel,
fosters us, smooths our hair, and brings us wild strawberries.*

**Instead of the testament I start and start, here. I've managed —**
I always manage *merely* — leafpiles, lists

of the lessonless: listenings, lessenings, losses and lusts.
My savoring you so insists the first

whisper (the first substitute for worlds enough and time) whisper
into the grace it whispers of: your mouth.

My love, your tongue unspools ells of tsujigahana-blushed silk
fit for gnarled, arthritic fingers to stitch.

Your mouth tastes of centuries-sunk bronze, incised with Aeschylus
(...*truth clings close*...), infused with Aegean salt.

Your mouth lasts *and* visits: bristlecone pine rooted in granite,
mountain bluebirds hovering over scrub.

It holds the hush dawn holds after *La Noche de Rábanos,*
pigeons in *el Zócalo,* murmuring.

Your lips feign two foxes frolicking through snow-dusted tallgrass,
entimbre grief as rosewood seconds spruce.

Though discovered in a desert cave, your vellum mouth maps me
a way through dense forest to waterfall.

**For a long time — months, even years — I expected a message:**
no one shuffles thus except visitants.

Along the streets of Laramie, a town with gulls overhead
but no waves alongside, a town of brown rock,

purple lilac, long shadows snarled by a fierce and frequent moon,
a man in a red jacket walks. Always.

He never speaks to others, but I have seen him muttering
into his thistly beard, tobacco-stained,

snot-stiff. The tremor when trains bellow north does not register
on his face or in his gait or posture.

In winter he adds a ski cap and blackened leather work gloves;
summers, opens two snaps of the jacket.

Out past town, pronghorn walk in lines. Some days, gray rain beards blue clouds
off to the west, but does not quite reach ground.

**By the way, about pain:**
We may distinguish it from suffering.
One might pass decades watching, each spring,
dogwood blossoms shimmer in sunlight
as though they themselves were suns,
without knowing that, too, they glow,
one with the moon.  Soon, though,
or late, crisis may impose a sleeplessness
that enforces one's seeing, as the sleepless see,
a spectral silver infusing everything.

**Halves or wholes, this songbird's spent selves?  One question or two they ask?**
One smears sunrise, unsouled soul ensouled, stilled

above its sister, disembodied body, eyes lost first, feet curled.
No concept of glass, just this strict practice.

Ants assess the mass abandoned to this old for some new world.
Through what plane did it, might they, must I, pass?

**By the way, about loss:**
Last frost past, I planted want
among the pitchpeas and crested squash
and Tentativity beets.  I wanted what
the heavens forbade, because they forbade it.
I bore the bucket back and forth,
despite my sense that thirst
tested *me* most, not this obstinate seedwaste.

**In that place, that time, when one season might subtend another,**
a man happened on an abandoned cap

buried all but its bill in snow drifted so that no one forget that cold,
though it start late, might tyrant yet into summer.

He took the cap for one he'd worn one then that then had still seemed now.
The cap felt dull and scuffed enough to match

an else half buried in that else-snow two halves cold, one half light:
those days in that city of knees his knees

touched, or thought they could touch, or tried to, under café tables,
eyes his eyes once matched through rising steam-scrim.

These days, though, the sky sent him its notes, such notes as it sent, only
through snow whose crystals skimmed morning sunlight

for their attempts to match the scattered stars as he, wandering,
sought from each clear dark sky the steadiness

of constellations impassive to cold however constant,
indifferent to space however vast.

**Divide towns if you think it matters into dead and dying.**
Needles brown down, beetle holes weep sap.

In the selvage of the light that fringes my brittle vision
I see movement but do not see what moves.

Those doves' coos I call *plaintive* are *incessant.* In some small towns
you still can see where once the station stood.

Surrounding some abandoned stations, you still can see ruins
of a town.  Some white clapboard chapels

knew no town, even back when, only ever knew a few stones'
moss-sloppy solace, know now to solicit

nothing else.  One no longer finds paths through stands of old growth
or paths across meadows, past beaver ponds,

but where else pass than along such paths, or even once-were-paths.
It should not grieve me but it does, the fact

that I am neither known where I will rest today, nor remembered
where I slept last night.  If not paint-peeled siding,

then I am rusting windmill.  If not burned down or just joist-sunk,
then boarded up.  If not husk, then withering.

**By the way, about pain, a question:**
Why *this* pain, not some other?
Why on this day, brought by this letter?
A minute either way, one beer more
or less, one more joke with the bartender,
and there had been no "other driver."

Why *this* pain, not some other?
White gloves, folded flag, burial with honor.
Why so great a pain, why not some lesser?
Why then?  Why in just that way?  Why *there*?
Will this pain be mine forever?
Will it stay *this* pain, not become some other?

**I am not alone in taking everything for messages.**
A man in love curves through the above

as a whale rills through the below, slow as though lumbering,
but so wholly, with so whole a body,

that in fulfilling purpose his progress animates grace.
Though in such depths the darkness and cold

be equally utter, he swims as would anyone sainted
by wave-fractured radiance.  All hum and trill,

he fills the very ocean, insists of the Vast that it listen.
A man in love blurs outlines, diffuses light,

lingers dense and indifferent as sea fog or forest mist,
merging a skeletoned ship with the sandbar

toward which it lists, and into which, slower, slowest, it sinks.
A man in love knows better than to ask

who abandoned the ship, understanding as he always has
each last lost cause.  In the forest nothing moves,

but each least click and whistle swells, as all calls all to all else.
A man in love makes magnets swim, can scrim

image without blighting light, invites to him the timid
and tetchy, tells most that won't to all that will.

A man in love meanders, sowing.  Apple seeds, wildflowers,
acorns.  On his knees with his own fingers

in moist mossed humus he digs, or upright with arcing gestures
scatters last year's litters and leavings across

this year's clodded rows. Or with his heel breaks up the caked dust.
A man in love, all plumb line and angle,

measures and rights, all alidade and abacus, all template
and quadrant and tally. A man in love

figures, accurate to many decimals. He plots and trues,
he registers and surveys and levels.

Hungry from his months of hibernation, a man in love
snuffs and muzzles a meadow's abundance,

browsing for berries and spiders and ants, digging for grubs,
grazing mountain greenery and blossoms,

savoring a winter's worth of clustered pellets of scat. His sight
is suspect, so he rears once or twice

to raise to the breeze his ears and muzzle, to listen and sniff.
Otherwise, all fours, lazily, nose first.

**From question to vision to lie, from curse to riddle and back.**
From a flicker hawk-struck, starved, or fallen

to a cat, three patterned primaries have blown into my yard.
Or were the other feathers blown away?

For lack of water, certainly, but not for lack of sunlight.
Issue your dictates, as did Creon his.

To reflect off this oily puddle, light has travelled how far?
I call you by the wrong name on purpose.

**By the way, about loss:**
How could I not wish now
that she had loved me then
a little more, a little less?
I could have imagined the worst
had I understood better.
Of what use is one love unless
to anticipate a next?

**Divide woods if you must into sanded smooth and smoothed by wear.**
Because they share the table, the woman

and the man clear it after each use. She leaves the surface clean:
barely shadowed by her favorite pen

or the leather-bound journal, the tenth at least he's given her,
on which each time before she opens it

she rests one hand one moment in pledge. Nor does he leave shavings
from the pencils he sharpens one by one

over end-torn envelopes and corner-torn sheets with a penknife
engraved with his grandfather's initials.

Neither knows that before they worked at this table a woman
ate simple meals from it alone each day

for half a century after her husband of two months left
to fight someone else's war, left for good.

For its part, the table knows nothing, asks no questions, receives
indifferently her journal or his

scrap copies, as it had the hand-me-down dinnerware that stood
first for hope, then in place of memory.

**By the way, about pain**
I state here the obvious:
It may visit suddenly, from outside,
or swell insistently within.
It may replace something lost:
a leg, a teenage daughter.
It may be trivial and accidental,
a fingertip sliced in the kitchen,
or may realize and localize
(electrocution of an "enemy combatant")
whole histories of hatred, global greeds.
My not wanting, not choosing, to inflict it
does not prevent my complicity.

I can state the obvious, thus,
but I can as easily lie:
*They deserve it.*
*It will be over soon.*
*Without it, we could not experience pleasure.*
*We will be free of it in heaven.*
*Its visits to the innocent fulfill God's plan.*
*We deserve it.*
*Those who inflict it on others*
*will have it inflicted on them.*
*There is a reason for it.*
*It will be over soon.*

**Back then I took things as messages I yet might understand,**
but sunlight now just settles, so much silt.

Now a man unloads angle iron, with each piece adjusting
his awkward stance, tenuously balanced

atop the unstable stack, one of three aboard a bowed flatbed.
A scuffed hard hat secures over his head

his sweatshirt hood.  From here he appears to be bantering with
the man to whom he hands each piece, the way

their hard hats tilt and bob out of sync with their rhythmic movements,
the way a third man turns to them, pausing

before adding a translucent trash bag to a dumpster stuffed
with lumber scraps and broken-down boxes.

Fifteen floors up, men in a line on a long metal scaffold
with bright orange safety netting along

its length glue four-foot squares of styrofoam to the building's side.
Not far from the levelled truck, five men stand,

each wearing an orange vest, one holding a styrofoam cup
from which once in a while he sips.  Above,

above the line of shadows cast by other buildings, the sun
makes the sheath of white insulation shine.

**By the way, about loss:**
Here.  Hold to your ear this
that I have held to mine.
Expect nothing.
Except you hear a sea.

**From question to vision to lie, from curse to riddle and back.**
Why the pause at windows?  Why trust vistas?

Complaints walls make in wind are not complaints about wind.  *You're asking for trouble.  Don't say I didn't warn you.*

On walls, anything not a window will pretend to be one.
*You look* at *only when you can't look* through.

Who says windows can't lie?  As when they say *light* but mean *surface.*
*Think what it says about you, this fear of depth.*

**Divide fetishes if you can into those that bind and those that spell.**
I wanted to be eggshell blue, thumbnail small,

a disk of Egyptian faience with a hole in the middle,
first lost under sand for three thousand summers,

later looted and smuggled and fenced, just so I could be sold
to one defeated lover to give

to an unfaithful other, because she to whom I was given
would wear the fragment on a chain as a charm.

It would rest against her breast, and she would test it absently
with her fingers at moments of distraction,

while she thought as a lover thinks who need not think, when she wanted
as one wants in moments of satisfaction.

**By the way, about fear:**
I didn't *mean* to fall away.
I own no whit of defiance.
I am, though, afraid of *everything.*
Others keep a lucky amulet
attached to their key chain, or,
on a necklace they wear every day,
a ring from a lover. I have my fear.
I carry it in my left front pocket,
always, because (of course)
I am afraid to leave it behind.
I couldn't carry it with me like this
without naming it, so I call it Kasimir,
because it resembles a nobleman
out of Chekhov, with serfs who scythe
his sazhens and sazhens of wheat,
but for whom each season it proves
harder and harder to find credit,
and whose estate falls each year
further, more utterly, into disrepair.
I talk to myself, out loud, when no one
is near (and no one ever is).
*How could they not distrust you,*
*you who cannot look yourself in the eye?*
*Even in school your fear was visible,*
*and gave away to Miss Cassandra*
*the failures she rightly foretold.*
So I slip through the party,
shuffling sideways, with my arms
above my head to avoid bumping
an elbow that would slosh someone's drink,
hoping only to get out the door
without Whoever Notices noticing.

**One question they pose, or two?  Attention, child of appetite,**
appetite child of delay.  Night consumes night,

one love another.  Those waking nights, who knew — you? — I waited,
hungry for this moonlight, and you moonlit?

**By the way, about absence:**
I did not beg that you not leave,
and do not plead that you return,
but when you do, my love of loves,
wander first the weed-wasted streets
of this abandoned town, filling in
from memory the smell of woodsmoke,
the rasp of snowgrit underfoot.
Once you *have* stood here
within what once were walls,
facing the west we so often wisted
through what then were windows,
scribble something on some scrap,
sign it with someone else's name,
and leave it for the wind to misdeliver,
so that, though I will not return,
each time I wish I could
I may embrace your absence with my own.

**In that place, that time, one season might have been any other.**
The house marked the shut-down of a short road

that ciphered the says-who of a long. The long road stopped short
(and started), the short road started (and stopped)

at the base of a hill, a ridge really, oblong and awkward,
the gangly second-grader embarrassed

above her uniform classmates, rises hardly more than mounds.
The short road gave up at the ridge's crest.

Beyond, to the west, just trees, trees that together defined
the horizon, though no one tree touched it.

Every morning I drove the long road. Every evening
I walked the short one, watched by wary deer.

Every night wind shook the house until it felt it might fall.
In that house, in*side,* just the one season,

but around it — garden, roads, woods — a million small transitions
nudged each last season out, each next one in.

That one spring, I surprised a field mouse nursing her blind hungers
under a canna leaf that all winter

had softened under snow, dyeing itself a black-soaked umber
to match the mud. Thus spring visited there:

hesitant at first but at last insistent, it threw its fits,
storms that boasted in the west, invective

issued in thunder and gusts, realized as lightning and hail.
That house that season was inhabited,

though I was not. That house that year was not haunted, but I was.
The creek tendered cattails, pebbles, turtles.

The cattails issued redwings and also lent their raspy voice
to the breeze the blackbirds animated.

That house was bounded by water, but I never knelt to it
and cupped my hands, never once waded in.

Goldfinches gloried by, glinting. Why not mythologize them?
Show me a god more luminous in flight.

The truths most necessary least suffice. My loves that spring all
were impossible. I wore a jacket

on those walks, but the sun and breeze conspired to keep my cheeks pink.
My cheeks, my earlobes, the bridge of my nose.

**By the way, about pain:**
As we see not the wind itself
but arcing treetops and waving grasses,
so in place of pain itself we see
flies crawling the infant's lips and eyes,
burns across a face and down a neck,
eyes shut and jaw set in a grimace,
arms extended forward from a body falling back.

**As if she were waiting for a message she might understand,**
a driver waits in her idling car,

first in a line stopped where a stretch of highway narrows to one lane
for repair of the other. It is dawn,

the horizon still a seam, the sky still heavy as its twin.
Yesterday she had a passenger. Today, not.

The men have arrived — the workers are all men — but not yet
set to work. They cluster in small groups,

not facing one another but looking off toward the low hills
or down at the graveled mud. Snowflakes

hospice briefly on their boots. The leather of those boots is dark
and heavy, not yet dried from yesterday.

Steam rises from the styrofoam cups they hold with both hands.
Each man wears a hooded sweatshirt under

and a jacket over canvas coveralls. Just before
the opposing line of cars passes,

one of the men gestures animatedly enough to spill
his coffee, and in his group the others laugh.

**From question to vision to lie, from curse to riddle and back.**
What's better, bargained over or fought for?

Your story sounded less false in someone else's telling it.
He treats you better, he paid more for you.

Footprints or fossil fish?  Keep digging, you won't reach water here.
In more ways than one, my thirst exceeds yours.

**By the way, about loss:**
Why not name it *creosote* instead,
or *chrysalis* or *incarnadine*?
Think what declarations might follow,
what pledges prove possible.
*I am cinders and whiplash.*
*Braced against what gust soever,*
*I assent to any season you assert.*
*Bless you, blood-red bird dead in snow.*

**Divide birds if you can into those that sing and those that cry.**
Though its song bring joy, no bird sings but from need.

The same pear blossoms that assert spring's start insinuate its end.
The waxwings just pass through, don't get attached.

Their stories swelled, yes, but those early sailors *had* seen monsters,
and the storms they survived followed them home.

Each leaves youth behind, Wyoming, all these young women and men
laying down their years here, piling them like pelts.

Had you cities, even one, some of these crows could be pigeons.
A bird's song washes the wind its flight charts.

Any song could assert hunger, sounded from such hollowness.
The gravity song transcends, flight dismisses.

Such preening would attract cupped hands even to one without wings.
Why do *we* sing, we torpid, flightless things?

**By the way, about pain,**
I don't speak here for others,
but for myself I pronounce this curse:
*Damn you, Source of pain.*
*Damn you, any occasion of it.*
*Damn you, least pain along with greatest.*
*Damn you, cancers of all kinds.*
*Damn you, arthritis, slipped disk, migraine, sciatica.*
*Damn you, accidents in mines and factories,*
*accidents on farms, on highways.*
*Damn you, torture and terror both,*
*wars by governments and wars against them.*
*Damn you, phantom limbs and phobias.*
*Damn you, all that men, after drink, do to women.*
*Damn you, falls down stairs*
*and falls on ice-slick sidewalks.*

**In this place, this time, one season overwhelms all others.**
Sparrows scatter when the merlin poses

atop my privacy fence.  For that matter, when I open
the storm door.  Where I sit now a man once stood

to curry his horse, following each brush stroke across her flank
with his other hand.  This is wind country,

creekbed country, country of cold nights.  Don't think that first mild day
in April will mean the end of snow.

**I expected messages for so long that now anything**
might hold secrets, might be an oracle.

Here, a husk once housefly, dry on a sill in brittle sunlight.
Here, a two-summers-past nest, first shred-built,

finally frost-shredded.  Here, down wisped from a not-to-return.
Here, now, how could I not relive how then

and for all you left, lifting off, first of a flock from a freezing lake,
rising past harvest row, over leaf-fall.

**One question that they pose, these words more shadow than word, or two?**
*They* began to speak as if to me

at just the moment *you* first spoke to me, and through all those years
between your saying to me what anyone

might say to anyone else and your saying what only you
could say only then and only to me

they followed me, those urgencies that though they could not be
spoken *by* were spoken *in* and *as* your voice.

*This wind contests, as any wind would,*
*the river's definition of the gorge.*

*These crystal specks glint in sunlight as if*
*the rock face were wet and they the water.*

*Who knows which the wind here rouses first,*
*those mountains or the clouds that mimic them.*

Though not whispered they were whispers. Though not words they were *of* words.
They were counterwords and I heard them

as at night one hears smaller shadows, shadows one cannot see,
skitter through larger shadows, shadows one can.

**I've meant, my love, to present you a testament. In its place,**
just this: I'll take lonely early mornings,

you take lonely snow-lit sidewalks. I'll keep bruises from a fall,
you keep blisters from a burn. Let's divide

this headlight-steadied world between us. Your lien on lightning leaves
wind-whipped whiteouts to me, your possessing

all patience leaves me to persist in sending out ships in search
of courage to claim. I'll take the slim stream

that must have as its source a spring because even in the parched
and parching months it flows cold as snowmelt,

you take the tall grasses that brown early and burr but secure
open stretches for this desiccant wind:

from the one and over the other rises a pair of ducks
from whose cramped, frantic wingbeats no one could

infer the elegant, synchronized curves their flight paths define.
I will continue scribbling my lists

and calculations, plotting maps of worlds, if-onlys inferred
from references to archives, fragments

of manuscripts of transcriptions of salt-told tall tales. You keep
your dreams, your murderous, merciless dreams.

# Books from Etruscan Press

*Zarathustra Must Die* | Dorian Alexander
*The Disappearance of Seth* | Kazim Ali
*Drift Ice* | Jennifer Atkinson
*Crow Man* | Tom Bailey
*Coronology* | Claire Bateman
*What We Ask of Flesh* | Remica L. Bingham
*The Greatest Jewish-American Lover in Hungarian History* | Michael Blumenthal
*No Hurry* | Michael Blumenthal
*Choir of the Wells* | Bruce Bond
*Cinder* | Bruce Bond
*Peal* | Bruce Bond
*Toucans in the Arctic* | Scott Coffel
*Body of a Dancer* | Renée E. D'Aoust
*Scything Grace* | Sean Thomas Dougherty
*Surrendering Oz* | Bonnie Friedman
*Nahoonkara* | Peter Grandbois
*Confessions of Doc Williams & Other Poems* | William Heyen
*The Football Corporations* | William Heyen
*A Poetics of Hiroshima* | William Heyen
*Shoah Train* | William Heyen
*September 11, 2001: American Writers Respond* | Edited by William Heyen
*As Easy As Lying* | H. L. Hix
*As Much As, If Not More Than* | H. L. Hix
*Chromatic* | H. L. Hix
*First Fire, Then Birds* | H. L. Hix
*God Bless* | H. L. Hix
*Incident Light* | H. L. Hix
*Legible Heavens* | H. L. Hix
*Lines of Inquiry* | H. L. Hix
*Shadows of Houses* | H. L. Hix
*Wild and Whirling Words: A Poetic Conversation* | Moderated by H. L. Hix
*Art Into Life* | Frederick R. Karl
*Free Concert: New and Selected Poems* | Milton Kessler
*Parallel Lives* | Michael Lind
*The Burning House* | Paul Lisicky
*Quick Kills* | Lynn Lurie
*Synergos* | Roberto Manzano
*The Subtle Bodies* | James McCorkle
*The Gambler's Nephew* | Jack Matthews

*An Archaeology of Yearning* | Bruce Mills
*Venison* | Thorpe Moeckel
*So Late, So Soon* | Carol Moldaw
*The Widening* | Carol Moldaw
*White Vespa* | Kevin Oderman
*The Shyster's Daughter* | Paula Priamos
*Help Wanted: Female* | Sara Pritchard
*American Amnesiac* | Diane Raptosh
*Saint Joe's Passion* | JD Schraffenberger
*Lies Will Take You Somewhere* | Sheila Schwartz
*Fast Animal* | Tim Seibles
*American Fugue* | Alexis Stamatis
*The Casanova Chronicles* | Myrna Stone
*The White Horse: A Colombian Journey* | Diane Thiel
*The Arsonist's Song Has Nothing to Do With Fire* | Allison Titus
*The Fugitive Self* | John Wheatcroft

# Etruscan Press Is Proud of Support Received From

Wilkes University

Youngstown State University

The Ohio Arts Council

The Stephen & Jeryl Oristaglio Foundation

The Nathalie & James Andrews Foundation

The National Endowment for the Arts

The Ruth H. Beecher Foundation

The Bates-Manzano Fund

The New Mexico Community Foundation

Drs. Barbara Brothers & Gratia Murphy Endowment

The Rayen Foundation

The Pella Foundation

Founded in 2001 with a generous grant from the Oristaglio Foundation, Etruscan Press is a nonprofit cooperative of poets and writers working to produce and promote books that nurture the dialogue among genres, achieve a distinctive voice, and reshape the literary and cultural histories of which we are a part.

etruscan press
www.etruscanpress.org

Etruscan Press books may be ordered from

Consortium Book Sales and Distribution
800.283.3572
www.cbsd.com

Small Press Distribution
800.869.7553
www.spdbooks.org

Etruscan Press is a 501(c)(3) nonprofit organization.
Contributions to Etruscan Press are tax deductible
as allowed under applicable law.
For more information, a prospectus,
or to order one of our titles,
contact us at books@etruscanpress.org.

CPSIA information can be obtained at www.ICGtesting.com
Printed in the USA
LVOW10s0747030815

448373LV00017B/16/P